SPARKS OF LIFE

Chemical Elements that Make Life Possible

HYDROGEN

by

Jean F. Blashfield

RSVP

RAINTREE
STECK-VAUGHN
PUBLISHERS
A Steck-Vaughn Company

Austin, Texas

Special thanks to our technical consultant,
Jeanne Hamers, Ph.D.,
formerly with the Institute of Chemical Education,
Madison, Wisconsin

Development: Books Two, Delavan, Wisconsin
       Graphics: Krueger Graphics, Janesville, Wisconsin
       Interior Design: Peg Esposito
       Photo Research and Indexing: Margie Benson

Raintree Steck-Vaughn Publisher's Staff:
       Publishing Director: Walter Kossmann   Project Editor: Frank Tarsitano
       Design Manager: Joyce Spicer   Electronic Production: Scott Melcer

Library of Congress Cataloging-in-Publication Data:
Blashfield, Jean F.
     Hydrogen / by Jean F. Blashfield.
       p. cm. — (Sparks of life)
     Includes bibliographical references (p. -) and index.
     Summary: Presents the basic concepts of this central element of the universe.
     ISBN 0-8172-5038-7
     1. Hydrogen — Juvenile literature. [1. Hydrogen.] I. Title. II. Series:
Blashfield, Jean F. Sparks of life.
QD181.01B52 1999   98-4524
546' .2 — dc21   CIP
                                    AC

Printed and bound in the United States.
 2 3 4 5 6 7 8 9 LB 03 02 01 00 99

PHOTO CREDITS: American Petroleum Institute 27; Archive Photos 11, 42, 52; ©Ballard Power Systems, Inc. (1997) 55, 57; Corbis-Bettmann 10, 40; B.I.F.C. cover; ©Ken Eward/Science Source 26; Courtesy Dr. Joanna S. Fowler/Brookhaven National Laboratory 50 both; Courtesy GE Medical Systems 48; Herd Seeder Co., Inc. 23; NASA cover, 8, 14; ©Alfred Pasieka/Science Photo Library 32; ©Timeframe Photography Inc./Photo Researchers 20; PhotoDisc, Inc. 38, 47; United Nations Photo 25; USDA, Soil Conservation Service 33; U.S. Geological Survey cover.

CONTENTS

Periodic Table of the Elements

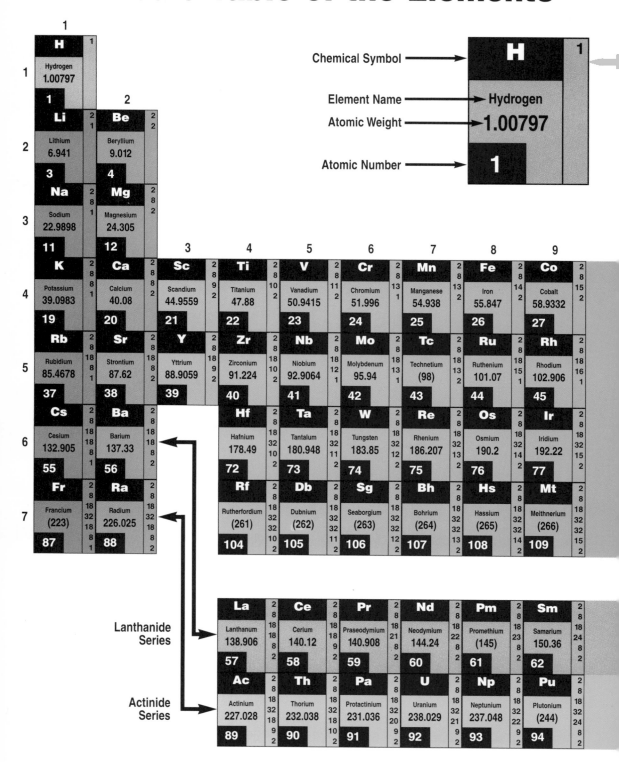

18

He 2
Helium
4.0026
2

Number of electrons in each shell,
beginning with the K shell, top.

See next page for explanations.

13	14	15	16	17	
B 2 3	**C** 2 4	**N** 2 5	**O** 2 6	**F** 2 7	**Ne** 2 8
Boron 10.81	Carbon 12.011	Nitrogen 14.0067	Oxygen 15.9994	Fluorine 18.9984	Neon 20.179
5	6	7	8	9	10
Al 2 8 3	**Si** 2 8 4	**P** 2 8 5	**S** 2 8 6	**Cl** 2 8 7	**Ar** 2 8 8
Aluminum 26.9815	Silicon 28.0855	Phosphorus 30.9738	Sulfur 32.06	Chlorine 35.453	Argon 39.948
13	14	15	16	17	18

10	11	12	13	14	15	16	17	18
Ni 2 8 16 2	**Cu** 2 8 18 1	**Zn** 2 8 18 2	**Ga** 2 8 18 3	**Ge** 2 8 18 4	**As** 2 8 18 5	**Se** 2 8 18 6	**Br** 2 8 18 7	**Kr** 2 8 18 8
Nickel 58.69	Copper 63.546	Zinc 65.39	Gallium 69.72	Germanium 72.59	Arsenic 74.9216	Selenium 78.96	Bromine 79.904	Krypton 83.80
28	29	30	31	32	33	34	35	36
Pd 2 8 18 18	**Ag** 2 8 18 18	**Cd** 2 8 18 18 1	**In** 2 8 18 18 3	**Sn** 2 8 18 18	**Sb** 2 8 18 18 5	**Te** 2 8 18 18	**I** 2 8 18 18	**Xe** 2 8 18 18 8
Palladium 106.42	Silver 107.868	Cadmium 112.41	Indium 114.82	Tin 118.71	Antimony 121.75	Tellurium 127.6	Iodine 126.905	Xenon 131.29
46	47	48	49	50	51	52	53	54
Pt 2 8 18 32 17 1	**Au** 2 8 18 32 1	**Hg** 2 8 18 32 18 2	**Tl** 2 8 18 32 18 3	**Pb** 2 8 18 32 18 4	**Bi** 2 8 18 32 18 5	**Po** 2 8 18 32 18 6	**At** 2 8 18 32 18 7	**Rn** 2 8 18 32 18 8
Platinum 195.08	Gold 196.967	Mercury 200.59	Thallium 204.383	Lead 207.2	Bismuth 208.98	Polonium (209)	Astatine (210)	Radon (222)
78	79	80	81	82	83	84	85	86
(Uun) 2 8 18 32 32 17 1	**(Unu)** 2 8 18 32 32 1	**(Uub)** 2 8 18 32 32 18 2						
(Ununnilium) (269)	(Unununium) (272)	(Ununbium) (277)						
110	111	112						

Alkali Metals
Transition Metals
Nonmetals
Metalloids
Lanthanide Series
Alkaline Earth Metals
Other Metals
Noble Gases
Actinide Series

COLOR KEYS

Eu 2 8 18 25 8 2	**Gd** 2 8 18 25 9 2	**Tb** 2 8 18 27 8 2	**Dy** 2 8 18 28 8 2	**Ho** 2 8 18 29 8 2	**Er** 2 8 18 30 8 2	**Tm** 2 8 18 31 8 2	**Yb** 2 8 18 32 8 2	**Lu** 2 8 18 32 9 2
Europium 151.96	Gadolinium 157.25	Terbium 158.925	Dysprosium 162.50	Holmium 164.93	Erbium 167.26	Thulium 168.934	Ytterbium 173.04	Lutetium 174.967
63	64	65	66	67	68	69	70	71
Am 2 8 18 32 25 8 2	**Cm** 2 8 18 32 25 9 2	**Bk** 2 8 18 32 26 9 2	**Cf** 2 8 18 32 28 8 2	**Es** 2 8 18 32 29 8 2	**Fm** 2 8 18 32 30 8 2	**Md** 2 8 18 32 31 8 2	**No** 2 8 18 32 32 8 2	**Lr** 2 8 18 32 32 9 2
Americium (243)	Curium (247)	Berkelium (247)	Californium (251)	Einsteinium (254)	Fermium (257)	Mendelevium (258)	Nobelium (259)	Lawrencium (260)
95	96	97	98	99	100	101	102	103

A Guide to the Periodic Table

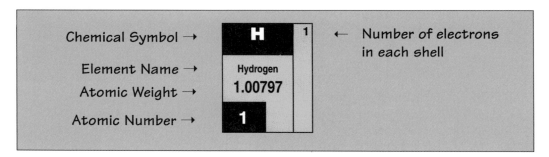

Chemical Symbol →

Element Name →

Atomic Weight →

Atomic Number →

← Number of electrons in each shell

H 1

Hydrogen

1.00797

1

Symbol = an abbreviation of an element name, agreed on by members of the International Union of Pure and Applied Chemistry. The idea to use symbols was started by a Swedish chemist, Jöns Jakob Berzelius, about 1814. Note that the elements with numbers 110, 111, and 112, which were "discovered" in 1996, have not yet been given official names.

Atomic number = the number of protons (particles with a positive charge) in the nucleus of an atom of an element; also equal to the number of electrons (particles with a negative charge) found in the shells, or rings, of an atom that does not have an electrical charge.

Atomic weight = the weight of an element compared to a standard element, carbon. When the Periodic Table was first developed, hydrogen was used as the standard. It was given an atomic weight of 1, but that created some difficulties, and in 1962, the standard was changed to carbon-12, which is the most common form of the element carbon, with an atomic weight of 12.

The Periodic Table on pages 4 and 5 shows the atomic weight of carbon as 12.011 because an atomic weight is an average of the weights, or masses, of all the different naturally occurring forms of an atom. Each form, called an isotope, has a different number of neutrons (uncharged particles) in the nucleus. Most elements have several isotopes, but chemists assume that any two samples of an element are made up of the same mixture of isotopes and thus have the same mass, or weight.

Electron shells = regions surrounding the nucleus of an atom in which the electrons move. Historically, electron shells have been described as orbits similar to a planet's orbit. But actually they are whole areas with a range of specific energy levels, in which certain electrons vibrate and move around. The shell closest to the nucleus, the K shell, can contain only 2 electrons. The K shell has the lowest energy level, and it is very hard to break its electrons away. The second shell, L, can contain only 8 electrons. Other shells may contain up to 32 electrons. The outer shell, in which chemical reactions occur, is called the valence shell.

Periods = horizontal rows of elements in the Periodic Table. A period contains all the elements with the same number of orbital shells of electrons. Note that the actinide and lanthanide (or rare earth) elements shown in rows below the main table really belong within the table, but it is not regarded as practical to print such a wide table as would be required.

Groups = vertical columns of elements in the Periodic Table, also called families. A group contains all elements that naturally have the same number of electrons in the outermost shell or orbital of the atom. Elements in a group tend to behave in similar ways.

Group 1 = alkali metals: very reactive and so never found in nature in their pure form. Bright, soft metals, they have one valence electron and conduct both electricity and heat.

Group 2 = alkaline earth metals: also very reactive and thus don't occur in their pure forms in nature. Harder and denser than alkali metals, they have two valence electrons that easily combine with other chemicals.

Groups 3–12 = transition metals: the great mass of metals, with a variable number of electrons; can exist in pure form.

Groups 13–17 = transition metals, metalloids, and nonmetals: Metalloids possess some characteristics of metals and some of nonmetals. Unlike metals and metalloids, nonmetals do not conduct electricity.

Group 18 = noble, or rare, gases: in general, these nonmetallic gaseous elements do not react with other elements because their valence shells are full.

"STINKING SMOKE" AND THE UNIVERSE

Many scientists think that stars and all other bodies in the universe began as a mass of swirling hydrogen.

Hydrogen is one of the most important elements in the universe and is thought to be the foundation of all matter. Many scientists believe that when our Milky Way first appeared about 15 billion years ago it was a mass of swirling hydrogen. Pockets of gas within the swirl gradually condensed, or shrank, into millions of stars. As these pockets condensed, the pressure within them created great heat, and temperatures rose high enough to allow the nucleus, or core, of one hydrogen atom to fuse to the nucleus of another. The resulting bigger nucleus was the core of a new element, helium (He, element #2). That process, which is called nuclear fusion, is still going on in the stars.

On Earth, it took many years for scientists to be sure that hydrogen was an element—a substance that cannot be broken down further without losing its distinctive characteristics. Centuries ago, alchemists—the early experimenters who blended science, magic, and religion—thought that the only elements were earth, air, fire, and water. They never considered that an invisible gas given off by various chemical reactions might be an element, one that we would later call hydrogen. The alchemists called the gas "vitriol of Mars." They usually knew it was being given off only because it sometimes caught fire.

Philippus Paracelsus, a Swiss scientist who lived 500 years ago, actually may have collected some of that gas, but if so, he didn't recognize that he had an element. In the mid-1600s, British scientist Robert Boyle collected the mysterious gas by dissolving iron (symbol Fe for the Latin name *ferrum;* element #26) in a strong acid. He called the gas "stinking smoke." He didn't recognize the gas as an element.

Trapped by Phlogiston

The problem was that alchemists were caught in the belief that many types of matter contained an invisible (and untrappable) substance. This substance wasn't hydrogen, but rather a mysterious "thing" in matter that was given off when the matter was burned.

This theory was proposed by Johann Joachim Becher, a German alchemist and physician in the mid-1600s. His student, Georg Ernst Stahl, made Becher's theory famous and gave the name phlogiston (meaning "able to be burned") to the mysterious substance.

Stahl's followers continued to try to prove the existence of phlogiston. They couldn't see it, or smell it, or capture it, but they were sure it was there. If, like Boyle, they put iron in a strong acid, they were certain that the invisible gas that issued forth was just another type of air. They didn't bother to investigate further because they were certain that the gas wasn't phlogiston, which was all they were interested in.

The Shy and the Bold

English chemist Henry Cavendish

Henry Cavendish was a wealthy English scientist who was so shy that he rarely spoke to other people. Even on those rare occasions when Cavendish did speak, he talked only to other scientists. But his colleagues recognized that Cavendish had a great mind, so they tolerated his eccentric behavior.

Cavendish owned several large houses, and he converted one of them into a huge laboratory for chemical experiments. About 1766, Cavendish was studying acids and deliberately collecting the invisible gas they gave off when reacting with metals. He described this gas (which we now know as hydrogen) accurately. He identified it as an element but called it "inflammable air." He mistakenly thought that it came from the metals, not recognizing that the hydrogen was actually given off by the acids.

This curious and eccentric researcher also collected his "inflammable air" in a container and mixed it with regular air. When he sent an electric spark through the mixture, it exploded, leaving liquid droplets on the sides of the container. Testing the droplets, Cavendish found that his small explosion had created water.

The story of the search for hydrogen then moved to France. Antoine Laurent Lavoisier was a French scientist who almost single-handedly

An artist of Lavoisier's time drew the French chemist as interested in collecting specimens.

turned alchemy into modern chemistry. He recorded every step he followed in a process and took nothing for granted. He also had the courage to question the treasured phlogiston theory. He investigated Cavendish's "inflammable air" and the process of combining it with "regular air."

Lavoisier is often credited with discovering oxygen (O, element #8), but Swedish chemist Carl Wilhelm Scheele and British researcher Joseph Priestley had identified that gas as an element in the 1770s. However, they both refused to give up the idea of phlogiston. Priestley called oxygen "dephlogisticated air."

Lavoisier named both oxygen and hydrogen. The name oxygen means "acid forming." He picked it because he thought that oxygen was present in all acids. However, he should have given that name to hydrogen since oxygen is not found in all acids, but hydrogen is. Lavoisier gave hydrogen its name because the word means "water forming." In German, hydrogen is still called *Wasserstoff*, or "water stuff."

Lavoisier performed many experiments with hydrogen and oxygen, often in front of fascinated audiences. The water produced by his first public demonstration of explosively combining the two elements is still preserved in a sealed bottle at the French Academy of Science in Paris.

THE PECULIAR ATOM

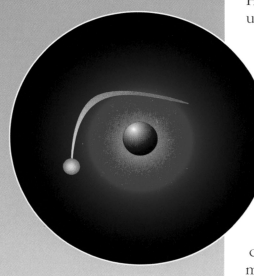

Hydrogen is the central element of the universe. About 76 percent of the universe is hydrogen by weight. In second place is helium, which makes up about 23 percent. Everything else in the entire universe—planets, plants, and people—fits into the other 1 percent.

An atom is often defined as the smallest particle of a substance. It is made up of a central nucleus consisting of protons, which have a positive electrical charge, and neutrons, which have no charge. Negatively charged electrons move around the nucleus.

Hydrogen is the exception to this and most other descriptions of elements. In fact, 99.98 percent of all hydrogen atoms do not have any neutrons at all. An atom of hydrogen consists of a single proton circled by a single electron. At normal temperatures, hydrogen is a tasteless, odorless, colorless gas.

Builder of the Universe

Many astronomers think that in the early days (or at least hours) of the formation of the universe, not all the elements we know today were present. In fact, they think that the exploding universe was too hot for any elements to exist. Perhaps protons and electrons existed freely and separately until a proton met up with an electron, and the first hydrogen atom was born.

Eventually, the protons of hydrogen atoms fused, and were joined by uncharged particles (neutrons), making up a new variety of nucleus. The result was helium, which has two protons and two neutrons in its nucleus, as well as two electrons in orbit around the nucleus. Hydrogen and helium were probably the only elements that existed until the nuclei of each fused into atoms of heavier elements.

The process of hydrogen changing into helium is the main way in which most stars—including our sun—burn. It takes four hydrogen atoms to fuse together in order to form one helium atom, but this reaction occurs only at about 10,000,000°C (18,000,000°F). When the temperature cools, this thermonuclear reaction ceases and gradually the star disappears.

When Earth first formed, its atmosphere contained mostly gaseous hydrogen. Many of our planet's rocks were formed early in its history, so a great deal of hydrogen was trapped in the rocks. Hydrogen is the tenth most abundant element in the Earth's crust, but because hydrogen is so light, it makes up only 0.1 percent of the Earth's weight.

Lightning makes hydrogen combine with oxygen, forming water. Over millions of years, Earth became the only water-covered planet in our solar system. Most free hydrogen disappeared. Now only about 0.00005 percent of our atmosphere is hydrogen.

Astronauts traveling in space can see for themselves that Earth's water gives it the nickname "Blue Planet."

Although the Earth is the only "water planet" in our solar system, several other planets have plenty of hydrogen. The main gas in Jupiter's atmosphere is free hydrogen. Scientists suspect that deep in the interior of that giant gaseous planet, the pressure is so high that the free hydrogen has probably condensed into a liquid metal. Saturn, the next planet beyond Jupiter, has an atmosphere that is a mixture of hydrogen and helium.

One of a Kind

As is fitting for the most basic and abundant element in the universe, hydrogen is unique. It is the only element whose properties could allow it to be put on both the right side and the left side of the Periodic Table. The elements on the left side form compounds by giving up electrons. Those on the right accept electrons in forming compounds. Hydrogen can do both.

When a hydrogen atom gives up its single electron to form a compound, it behaves as an electropositive element. That makes it belong to Group 1, along with sodium (Na, element #11), potassium (K, #19), and others found in the the first column of the Periodic Table. The process of giving up electrons is called reduction. Hydrogen can be used to reduce metal ores to their pure elements. Iron (Fe, element #26), mercury (Hg, #80), and copper (Cu, #29) can be separated from their ores by reduction carried out by hydrogen.

However, hydrogen can also capture another electron to form a compound. That makes it electronegative, like the Group 7 elements, which include fluorine (F, element #9), chlorine (Cl, #17), and other elements toward the right side of the Periodic Table. Taking electrons from another element is called oxidation. The process was originally seen as a trait of oxygen.

Because of its urge to react with other elements—its instability—pure hydrogen gas is not a collection of single atoms. It most often occurs in nature as a diatomic (or two-atomed) element. This means that free hydrogen (of which there isn't very much in our atmosphere) consists of molecules made up of two atoms of hydrogen sharing electrons so that each one has a filled outer shell. This kind of hydrogen—H_2—is stable. It has little tendency to react with other elements, except under special circumstances.

Two atoms of hydrogen join, forming a diatomic molecule. Each atom shares its electron with a second atom. Under normal conditions, diatomic hydrogen (H_2) will not react with other elements.

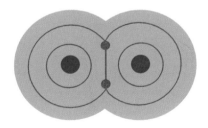

Oxygen is also a diatomic element. Hydrogen and oxygen in the air will react together to form water when an electric charge such as lightning provides the energy needed for the change to take place. It takes two molecules of diatomic hydrogen and one molecule of diatomic oxygen to make two molecules of water. However, by weight, hydrogen is so light that it makes up only 11 percent of water.

$$2H_2 + O_2 \rightarrow 2H_2O$$

Atoms have an "urge" to become stable, which means having their outer, or valence, shells (the region in which an electron moves) filled with as many electrons as this shell can hold. Atoms can do this by losing electrons, gaining electrons, or sharing electrons. As you can see in the diagram on the previous page, hydrogen molecules are formed when each of the two hydrogen atoms contributes one electron each to the molecule so that each individual atom has its only shell filled with two electrons.

Oxygen atoms also share electrons when they form diatomic molecules. An oxygen atom has two electron shells. Its second, or outer, shell has six electrons but can hold eight. For an oxygen atom to become stable, it must acquire two more electrons to fill the outer shell.

It seems odd that diatomic hydrogen, which is stable, and diatomic oxygen, which is also stable, react explosively to form water when an electrical charge goes through the gases. The reason this happens lies in the difference between the two kinds of molecules. The strength with which an oxygen atom pulls electrons toward it is strong enough to cause the hydrogen molecule to break apart and share its electrons. However, you could have a roomful of mixed hydrogen and oxygen gas and nothing will happen unless an electric spark is added.

There is a force called a hydrogen bond that is an attraction between a hydrogen atom in one molecule and a different atom—such as oxygen, nitrogen (N, element #7), or fluorine—in another molecule. This force holds molecules near each other.

Both liquid water and ice contain hydrogen bonds. A water molecule is bent, or lopsided, because of the way the two

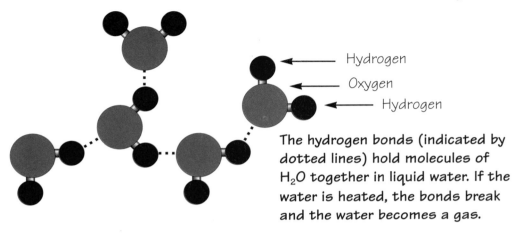

Hydrogen

Oxygen

Hydrogen

The hydrogen bonds (indicated by dotted lines) hold molecules of H₂O together in liquid water. If the water is heated, the bonds break and the water becomes a gas.

different kinds of atoms join. In liquid water, the molecules are held near each other by the hydrogen bonds. The attraction is not enough to chemically combine the atoms, but it is enough to keep the molecules close to each other. This bond makes water have a higher boiling point (100°C; 212°F) than many other liquids of similar molecular weights. The hydrogen bonds keep the molecules in liquid water from floating apart until the temperature is high enough to break the bonds.

The number of hydrogen bonds in water varies with temperature. In liquid water, the molecules are continually moving around, so hydrogen bonds come and go. If the temperature drops and the water freezes into ice, the hydrogen bonds hold all the molecules tightly together. If the temperature reaches boiling point, the molecules move too far apart for bonds to hold. The water turns into a gas, water vapor.

Without hydrogen bonds holding the molecules together as liquid, we would have no rivers, lakes, or oceans because all water would be a gas. And perhaps worst of all, there would be no water in our bodies, which are about 70 percent water. Life as we know it could not exist without hydrogen bonds.

When a molecule is very large (as in some plastics), hydrogen bonds can form between atoms on different parts of the molecule. In deoxyribonucleic acid (DNA, the substance in living cells that carries hereditary information), two different strands of molecules are hydrogen-bonded together to form the spiral molecule shown on the front cover of this book.

Hydrogen's Isotopes

Hydrogen exists in three forms, or isotopes. The word isotope means "same place," because all isotopes of an element occupy the same place in the Periodic Table. They differ only in the number of neutrons in their nuclei. The most common form or isotope of hydrogen is called protium and is given the atomic weight, or mass number, of 1. A protium atom consists of one proton and one electron.

The hydrogen isotope that has a neutron in its nucleus along with the single proton is called deuterium, meaning "second." It makes up 0.015 percent of all natural hydrogen—that's only 1 in 6,700 atoms. Deuterium is also called heavy hydrogen, or H-2. It has an atomic weight, or mass number, of 2. Like H-1, deuterium exists as a diatomic gas. When it combines—explosively—with oxygen, it forms what is called heavy water. Because it is awkward to write heavy water as $H\text{-}2_2O$, deuterium is given its own symbol of D. Heavy water is then written as D_2O.

The existence of heavy hydrogen was suspected soon after English chemist Frederick Soddy proposed the idea of isotopes in 1913. However, at that time, no one could prove that heavy hydrogen existed.

In 1931, American chemist Harold Clayton Urey, working at Columbia University, discovered heavy hydrogen by recognizing that the electrons of some hydrogen atoms appeared to have more energy than most other hydrogen atoms. He received the 1934 Nobel Prize in Chemistry for this work.

A third form of hydrogen is tritium, which has two neutrons in its nucleus. It exists naturally in water but only in the tiniest

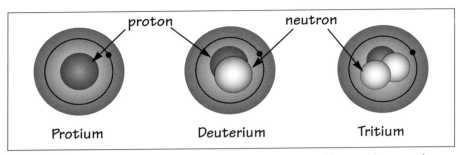

Protium   Deuterium   Tritium

Hydrogen has three forms, or isotopes. They differ in the number of neutrons found in the nucleus. The simplest hydrogen atom, protium, has no neutrons in its nucleus.

amounts—about one atom in 100,000,000,000,000,000 (100 quadrillion) molecules of water.

Tritium was manufactured artificially in 1934 by Australian physicist Marcus Oliphant by bombarding deuterium with its own nuclei (deuterons). Tritium can also be made by bombarding lithium (Li, element #3) with neutrons. Tritium, which has an atomic weight of 3 and is also called hydrogen-3, or H-3, is used in making the hydrogen bomb.

In developing the Periodic Table of the Elements, chemists working in the 1850s used one atom of hydrogen as the base against which the atomic weights (or masses) of all elements were compared. Hydrogen was given an atomic weight of 1 atomic mass unit (amu). The table was later revised to use an atom of the most abundant isotope of carbon—carbon-12—as the base. Carbon-12 was assigned an atomic weight of 12.0 amu. All other elements are assigned weights relative to this carbon-12 isotope.

The mass of protium (hydrogen-1) is about (but not exactly) one-twelfth that of carbon-12. Taken together, the three isotopes give hydrogen an overall atomic weight of 1.00797.

THE ACID MAKER

Hydrochloric acid (HCl) reacts with metallic zinc, releasing diatomic hydrogen gas.

Acids are chemicals that can be defined in several ways. One way to define acids is by describing their interesting and important properties. For instance, acids have a sour taste when they are in liquid form. But don't taste them even if you're sure they're safe. The juice in a grapefruit, for example, contains citric acid. **Acids should never be test-tasted. They can kill.**

Acids also burn when they touch the skin. Sometimes they burn only slightly. You wouldn't feel a tingly sensation if grapefruit juice or vinegar (which contains acetic acid) was dabbed on your skin but other acids can cause serious burns because they eat away, or corrode, other substances. You always must handle all acids carefully. Some acids are powerful enough to dissolve certain metals and—as alchemists discovered—give off a gas in the process. Imagine what those same acids can do to your flesh! So again—be careful around acids!

Chemists in a laboratory use a special paper called litmus paper to see if a liquid is an acid. Acids make litmus paper turn red.

To chemists, acids are defined most simply as substances that give up hydrogen ions when dissolved in water. An ion is an atom or group of atoms that has an electrical charge because it does not have an equal number of electrons and protons. The charge is positive when the ion has more protons than electrons and negative when it has fewer protons than electrons.

A hydrogen atom has only one electron, so if it loses an electron, it's left with only a positive nucleus, or proton. That particular ion is written H^+. The stronger an acid is, the more hydrogen ions it gives off when dissolved in water.

pH

Another definition of an acid is that it is a substance with a pH below 7. The abbreviation pH stands for "potential of hydrogen." It represents the concentration of hydrogen ions in a solution. The pH scale, which goes from 0 to 14, was devised by a Dane, Søren Sørensen, in 1909.

Each number on the pH scale means that the liquid is ten times more or less acidic than the previous number. The closer to zero a solution is on the scale, the more acidic it is—that is, the greater the concentration of H^+ ions. The midpoint of the scale—7—is neutral. Distilled water is neutral, and our blood is nearly 7.

THE pH SCALE

STRONG ACID

Battery acid	1	Hydro-chloric acid
Vinegar	2	Lemon
	3	Apples
	4	Wine
Acid rain		
	5	
Normal rain		Urine
	6	Milk
Pure water	7	Human blood
Seawater	8	Egg
	9	
Soap	10	Milk of Magnesia
Ammonia	11	
	12	
Lime (CaO)		
	13	
Lye	14	

STRONG BASE

Substances above 7 are called bases. They are described as being alkaline, or basic. Bases are chemical opposites of acids. When dissolved in water, they increase the concentration of a different kind of partial molecule, called a hydroxyl ion and written OH-. The hydroxyl ion from a base has an extra electron and therefore has a negative electrical charge. It readily combines with a positive hydrogen ion from an acid to form a neutral molecule—water. This is how a base neutralizes an acid.

Soap and baking soda are common bases. The strongest base we use in daily life is sodium hydroxide (NaOH), used in chemical products that clear clogged drains. These products work by dissolving whatever material is plugging up drainage pipes.

With Carbon and Without

Acids that contain the element carbon (C, element #6) are called organic acids. The citric acid found in grapefruit and other citrus fruits has the chemical formula $C_6H_8O_7$. Acetylsalicylic acid, better known as aspirin, is $C_9H_8O_4$. Acetic acid, which is found in vinegar, is $C_2H_4O_2$.

Acids without carbon are called inorganic, or mineral, acids. Oddly enough, one of the most important inorganic acids is found in our very organic bodies—hydrochloric acid (HCl). Also called muriatic acid, it is very powerful and even poisonous, but it is found in very tiny amounts in the stomach. Up to half of 1 percent of the digestive juices of human beings is hydrochloric acid, which aids in digestion.

Scientists were stunned when they realized this. They were unable to understand how hydrochloric acid, which is very strong, didn't eat away the stomach lining. Further study showed that the stomach secretes a fluid, or mucus, that coats the stomach and does not react to the acid. However, that protective mucus does not extend up into the bottom of the throat, or esophagus. Some foods, or even stress, can cause the acid to rise up into the esophagus. A person experiences acid in the esophagus as the painful, sour-tasting condition called heartburn.

Several different chemicals are useful in combating heartburn. All it takes is something that combines with the hydrogen ions and neutralizes the acid. The oldest antacid is sodium bicarbonate ($NaHCO_3$), which works as follows:

$$NaHCO_3 + HCl \rightarrow NaCl + H_2O + CO_2$$

The NaCl is common, ordinary salt, and the other two products are water and carbon dioxide.

Acids in the human body are not limited to the stomach. The pH of plaque, the substance that can build up around teeth, is quite low, meaning there are many hydrogen ions in the mouth. These hydrogen ions prevent the buildup of new mineral in the teeth. New mineral is needed to keep teeth strong because it is continually lost. Teeth need to be brushed frequently to prevent the buildup of plaque.

Acids in Soil

Soils can be acidic or basic (alkaline), depending usually on the minerals they contain or the type of plants that have been grown or are presently growing in the soils. Prairie soils, for example, are usually basic while the soil in pine forests is acidic.

Most plants will usually grow to some extent in either acidic or alkaline soil, but they do better in one type or the other. Some

This field of blueberry bushes is being sprayed with an acidic fertilizer at the start of the growing season in order to encourage the fruit to grow.

plants produce sweeter fruit if their soil is slightly alkaline. Blueberry bushes can grow in either acidic or alkaline soil, but they will produce fruit only in the former.

Farmers who want to change the kind of crops they grow may also have to change the pH of their soil. Potatoes need a lot of acid, while wheat and corn need comparatively less. Altering the quality of soil isn't as difficult as one might think. For example, limestone, which is calcium carbonate ($CaCO_3$), can be sprinkled into an acidic soil to bring the pH closer to neutral.

Putting Acids to Work

Acids used on an industrial level are generally very powerful. They are used to break down other chemicals, to refine metals, and as ingredients in the production of plastics, paints, fertilizers, and explosives.

Sulfuric acid (H_2SO_4)—sulfur is S, element #16—is used in refining petroleum, making fertilizers and detergents, and in producing electricity in car batteries. Sulfuric acid was the first acid produced commercially in the United States. Its many uses make it the most commonly produced acid in the United States.

Hydrocyanic acid (HCN) is hydrogen cyanide dissolved in water. One of the most poisonous substances known, it has sometimes been used to execute criminals. Cassava, one of the main starch-producing plants in Africa and South America, can be converted by stomach acid into hydrogen cyanide. People who eat cassava must first grind up the flesh of the root, wash it, and wash it again before cooking it.

Because hydrofluoric acid (HF) eats into, or corrodes, glass, this acid is used for etching designs on glass. Nitric acid (HNO_3), which reacts easily with other substances, is useful for producing other chemicals and in the manufacture of synthetic textiles such as polyester. Phosphoric acid (H_3PO_4) is used in refining sugar, making carbonated drinks, and in printing.

These women in an African country must prepare cassava by pounding and then washing it to remove the compounds that can become toxic.

Acids for Life

Proteins, which are often considered the main building blocks of life, are huge molecules made up of special organic acids called amino acids. There are twenty different amino acids in the human body. Some of them are produced by the body itself, but others, called essential amino acids, must be obtained from protein-rich food. Some essential amino acids are obtained from meats and some from vegetables. A vegetarian—a person who chooses not to eat meat—must be sure to eat certain plant foods and/or milk in order to obtain the essential amino acids.

All amino acids contain a group of atoms called an amino group. An amino group consists of two hydrogen atoms and one nitrogen atom. It is written —NH_2. Amino acids also contain a carboxylic group, which consists of a carbon atom, two oxygen atoms, and a hydrogen atom. It is written —COOH.

Two other kinds of organic acids help determine the genetic structure of organisms. These acids, called nucleic acids, are found in all living cells. One kind, called ribonucleic acid (RNA), exists outside the nucleus of the cell. It provides the instructions for the cell to construct proteins from amino acids. The RNA gets its instructions from another acid, deoxyribonucleic acid (DNA). This acid is located primarily inside the nucleus of cells in the chromosomes, which contain hereditary information, or genes.

Nucleic acids are constructed of many huge molecules called nucleotides. Hydrogen atoms are located along the outer parts of these complex nucleotide molecules. When the hydrogen atoms lie near nitrogen or oxygen in an adjacent molecule, a hydrogen bond forms, holding the molecule pairs together. Such hydrogen bonds make the big nucleic acid molecules curve into what is called the double-helix shape. A double helix consists of two intertwining spirals, as shown in the molecular model of DNA below.

No two people have exactly the same DNA structure. That uniqueness lets scientists use DNA in hair or blood left at a crime scene to find out whether a person might have committed a crime. DNA can also be used to determine whether a person can possibly be the parent of another. But, amazingly, the millions upon millions of possible DNA combinations are all constructed from only four different kinds of nucleotides.

A computer-generated model of a DNA (deoxyribonucleic acid) molecule shows its spiral, or double-helix, shape. The huge molecule is made up of many smaller submolecules.

ORGANIC COMPOUNDS: MOLECULES OF LIFE

Organic chemistry is the branch of chemistry that deals strictly with compounds made up of carbon and other elements, such as hydrogen, oxygen, and nitrogen. At one time scientists thought that only living things (organisms) could produce organic compounds. We now know better. Some organic compounds can be made in laboratories.

Among the most significant organic compounds in our lives, however, are those that originated as living things. These compounds, are called hydrocarbons and they consist only of carbon and hydrogen atoms. There are very many hydrocarbon compounds in our world.

Petroleum being pumped from beneath the sea by this off-shore oil rig is a mixture of organic compounds derived from plants and animals.

Hydrocarbons

Hydrocarbons are the primary compounds found in petroleum and natural gas. We burn such hydrocarbons for heat; we drive vehicles powered by them; and we rearrange their molecules in order to make numerous materials, including plastics.

Petroleum and natural gas are called fossil fuels because they are made from the remains of vast numbers of plants and animals that died millions of years ago. Over time, these remains were changed under great heat and pressure into fuels.

Petroleum and natural gas are not single substances. They are complex mixtures of many different hydrocarbons. The simplest hydrocarbon in natural gas is methane (CH_4).

Carbon is a tetravalent atom, meaning that it needs to obtain four (*tetra* means "four") more electrons in order to reach the total of eight electrons carbon can hold in its outer, or valence, shell. Hydrogen is *mono*valent, meaning that it requires only one more electron to have a filled outer shell. Therefore, methane—with one carbon bonded to four hydrogen atoms—is as simple as a hydrocarbon can be.

Gaining Complexity—Structural Formulas

After methane, the next most complicated hydrocarbon is ethane. Instead of one carbon atom, it has two. Its chemical formula is C_2H_6. But it is more often written as CH_3CH_3. The second way of writing the formula shows something about the molecule's structure or the way the atoms are arranged. It shows that two groups of atoms—each consisting of a carbon atom and three hydrogen atoms—are attached to each other.

Chemists are just as interested in the arrangement of atoms in an organic molecule as they are in the molecule's atomic makeup. They use a special notation called a structural formula to show how the atoms are arranged. In a structural formula, chemical symbols of the atoms are arranged as the atoms are found in the actual molecule.

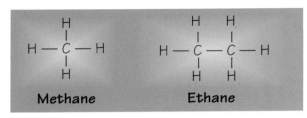

Methane   **Ethane**

Structures of the two simplest hydrocarbons

Methane's structural formula, for example, is shown at the left in the diagram. A single line (vertical or horizontal) represents a single bond. In the structural formula of ethane, on the right, you can see that each carbon atom is attached to three hydrogen atoms and an additional carbon atom.

Methane and ethane are the first two hydrocarbons in a series called alkanes. Each succeeding alkane in the series gets larger and larger with the addition of CH_2 groups in between the CH_3 groups. Propane, a gas commonly used for heating, for example, could be written $CH_3CH_2CH_3$.

Other series of hydrocarbons still contain only carbon and hydrogen but they are combined differently. The carbon atoms in alkanes share only one pair of electrons. But in a series called the alkenes, the carbon atoms share two pairs of electrons, which is indicated by two lines connecting the carbon atoms. The simplest alkene, shown at the right, is the gas called ethylene, C_2H_4.

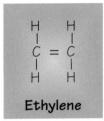

Ethylene

As each series of hydrocarbon molecules increase in complexity, the boiling points of the series rise, as do the melting points. A chemical called triacontane, for example, which consists of twenty-eight CH_2 groups plus two CH_3 groups, has a boiling point of 450°C (842°F) and a melting point of 66°C (151°F). In addition, the larger the molecule, the thicker the fluid. Methane is a gas, while, on the other hand, triacontane is a thick, sludgy material used in asphalt.

In addition to hydrocarbons, there are many other kinds of organic compounds. These other compounds may contain atoms of other elements such as oxygen or nitrogen in addition to carbon and hydrogen. For example, compounds that contain an —OH group of atoms are called alcohols.

Isomers

Organic compounds of various kinds can have the same chemical formula but different arrangements of atoms. Such chemicals are called isomers. For example, two different chemicals—ethyl alcohol and dimethyl ether—have the standard chemical formula C_2H_5O, so the chemical formula does not reveal which compound is which. Their structural formulas, however, illustrate how the atoms are organized, which shows how they are different.

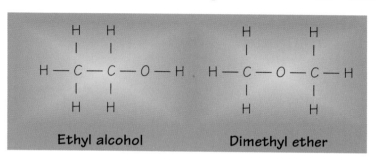

Ethyl alcohol   Dimethyl ether

The structural formula shown on the far left is for ethyl alcohol, or ethanol, which is a liquid. It is the type of alcohol found in alcoholic beverages. It is also combined with gasoline to make the automotive fuel called gasohol. Ethyl alcohol boils at 78°C (172.4°F).

The structural formula on the right in the box above is for dimethyl ether, a gas. Dimethyl ether contains two atoms of carbon attached to one atom of oxygen.

Fats and Oils

One special category of organic compounds consists of fats and oils. Fats and oils are chemically similar. We sometimes call them by different names depending on whether or not they are liquid at room temperature. Technically, a fat can be either liquid or solid. Fat molecules are large and will not dissolve in water. Fats usually are derived from animals, and oils are usually derived from the seeds of plants.

Both plant and animal fats are the main energy-producing chemicals taken into our bodies. Fats provide more energy than either proteins or carbohydrates, which are the other two main ingredients in food.

Some fats contain a waxy substance called cholesterol. Cholesterol can accumulate inside the walls of the arteries in our bodies. This accumulation can be especially dangerous when it occurs in the arteries leading to the heart. You've probably seen advertisements emphasizing the importance of switching from butter to margarine, and in those ads, you may have read the terms "saturated," "unsaturated," and "polyunsaturated" fats.

What are saturated (meaning "filled") fats saturated with? Hydrogen atoms. Fats contain fatty acids, which are organic compounds made up of long chains of carbon and hydrogen atoms, along with some oxygen. In saturated fat, the carbon atoms that are not at the end of the chains are attached to at least two hydrogen atoms. These carbon atoms are filled up (saturated) with hydrogen atoms. They cannot hold any more hydrogen atoms.

In monounsaturated fats, two of the carbon atoms have room for one more hydrogen atom each. In polyunsaturated fats, three or more carbon atoms can each hold an additional hydrogen atom. This may seem like a very small difference, and yet this difference could be the line between someone having a healthy heart or not.

Saturated fatty acid   Polyunsaturated fatty acid

Butter is fat made from cow's milk. It is a naturally solid, saturated fat. Margarines, on the other hand, are made from naturally unsaturated or polyunsaturated oil plants such as soybeans, corn, or rapeseed, which produces canola oil. Contrary to what some people think, not all plant oils are safely unsaturated. Some oils of tropical origin, such as coconut oil and palm oil, are also saturated.

Plant oils are sometimes hardened to look like butter by artificially adding hydrogen atoms to the unsaturated fatty acid molecules. Adding hydrogen to unsaturated fats is called hydrogenation. If all of the hydrogen that could be added was added, the fat would become solid, like the fat on a marbled steak.

Some researchers think that artificially hydrogenated fats are just as bad for people as naturally saturated fats. Apparently the hydrogenation process produces trans-fatty acids that have the ability to both raise the amount of "bad" cholesterol (called LDL for low-density lipoproteins) in the blood (which produces plaque that clogs arteries) while reducing the amount of "good" cholesterol (HDL, or high-density lipoproteins—which carries plaque out of the arteries).

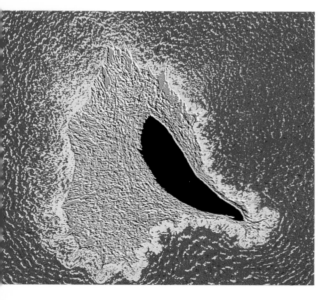

The buildup of cholesterol in arteries occurs as a substance called plaque (shown in white). The artery wall in this cross section is the red part. The plaque leaves only a small opening (black) for blood to flow through.

WATER WIZARDRY

Hydrogen and oxygen, when combined by the power of electricity, make water. Just as the process of combining the two elements to make water can be very useful, so can the process of taking water apart.

Taking Water Apart

Six years after Lavoisier's death in 1794, two English scientists, William Nicholson and Sir Anthony Carlisle, separated (or "decomposed") water into hydrogen and oxygen gases by running electricity through it. This process, called electrolysis, is often used today in laboratories to obtain small samples of the two gases.

During electrolysis, two metal rods, called electrodes, are submerged in water that contains a little salt. The salt is present

Water is an amazing substance that plays a role in all living things.

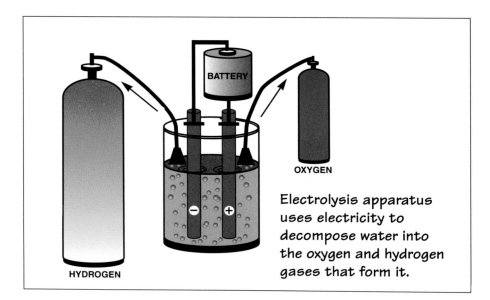

OXYGEN

Electrolysis apparatus uses electricity to decompose water into the oxygen and hydrogen gases that form it.

HYDROGEN

only to help conduct electricity through the water because pure water is not a good conductor.

When the electrodes are connected to a battery, the negative electrode gives up electrons to the fluid (in this case, water), or electrolyte. The positive electrode attracts negative ions from the electrolyte. The negative ions give up their extra electrons and become neutral again.

At the negative electrode, the water molecule takes up an extra electron, forming H_2 and hydroxyl ions: (In the following equations, e- means "electron.")

$$4H_2O + 4e^- \rightarrow 2H_2 + 4OH^-$$

At the positive electrode, the water molecule gives up some electrons and is broken down into oxygen gas (which bubbles off) and hydrogen ions:

$$2H_2O \rightarrow 4e^- + O_2 + 4H^+$$

Then the hydrogen ions and the hydroxyls form water, which can be broken down again:

$$4OH^- + 4H^+ \rightarrow 4H_2O$$

Together, all the reactions look like this:

$$2H_2O + \text{electricity} \rightarrow 2H_2 + O_2$$

Because water contains two hydrogen atoms for every oxygen atom, twice as much hydrogen as oxygen is given off.

Electrolysis can be used to break many substances down to their basic elements. Aluminum (Al, element #13) is separated from aluminum oxide (which is the aluminum ore called bauxite) in this way. And metal objects can be plated (have a thin layer of another metal added to their surfaces) when the objects serve as electrodes in an electrolytic process.

Commercial Hydrogen

Because of the cost of electricity, electrolysis is a very expensive way to obtain hydrogen gas. Therefore, electrolysis is used only in places where electricity does not cost much, such as near a dam where electric power is generated. Even then, the amount of energy available from the hydrogen produced is probably only one-fifth of the electrical energy used to produce it—not a practical solution!

Today, hydrogen is produced in industrial-sized amounts by removing it from fossil fuels. Petroleum and natural gas contain a great deal of hydrogen because they consist primarily of hydrocarbons. The major part of natural gas is methane, CH_4. This hydrocarbon can react with water (in the presence of a catalyst) to produce hydrogen and carbon dioxide:

$$CH_4 + 2H_2O \rightarrow CO_2 + 4H_2$$

In another method of obtaining hydrogen, carbon, in the form of coal or coke, has hot steam passed over it. The carbon and water react, turning into water gas, which is a combination of hydrogen and carbon monoxide:

$$H_2O + C \rightarrow CO + H_2$$

Water gas is also called blue gas because it burns with a blue flame. It can be used directly as fuel, although it is more likely to be used as a source of hydrogen.

Very small amounts of hydrogen can readily be obtained by treating a metal with hydrochloric acid. For example, when bits of metallic zinc (Zn, element #30) are placed in a test tube and hydrochloric acid is added, the hydrogen given off can be collected through a tube in the stopper. This is the reaction that occurs:

$$Zn + 2HCl \rightarrow H_2 + ZnCl_2$$

Putting Water Back Together—The Fuel Cell

A fuel cell is a device that works on the opposite principles of electrolysis. Instead of using electricity to separate the elements in water, it can, for example, combine hydrogen and

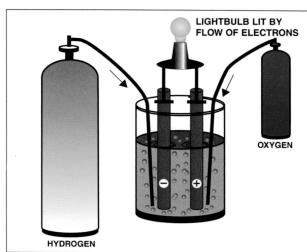

LIGHTBULB LIT BY
FLOW OF ELECTRONS

OXYGEN

HYDROGEN

The fuel cell that scientists hope will become practical in the future uses a reaction that is the opposite of electrolysis. It turns hydrogen and oxygen gases into ions that flow, producing electricity and water.

oxygen gases to make water. More importantly, this reaction produces energy in the form of electricity. Unlike other ways of producing electricity, there is no heat given off in the process.

The two gases are bubbled around electrodes that are submerged in a liquid bath that provides a catalyst—a chemical that participates in the reaction but not in the product. Potassium hydroxide is often used.

At the negative electrode, hydrogen combines with hydroxyl ions (produced at the other electrode), resulting in water and electrons:

$$2H_2 + 4OH^- \rightarrow 4H_2O + 4e\text{-}$$

The unattached electrons enter the electric circuit attached to the electrode. Then they do their work of powering an electric car or the electric equipment in manned space vehicles before going into the positive electrode.

At the positive electrode, oxygen combines with water and extra electrons to produce hydroxyl ions:

$$O_2 + 2H_2O + 4e\text{-} \rightarrow 4OH\text{-}$$

Together, the two processes are the opposite of electrolysis:

$$2H_2 + O_2 \rightarrow 2H_2O$$

Amazingly enough, the principles of the fuel cell were demonstrated as long ago as 1839 by Sir Robert Grove, a lawyer-turned-experimenter. But more than 150 years later, fuel cells are still not in regular use. They are seen as an important answer to creating engines that don't pollute the environment as gasoline engines do. So far, they are too bulky and expensive to use in cars.

An additional problem for the environment is the water vapor produced by the chemical reaction. If too many cars were producing too much water vapor, our weather could change, bringing more rain. Research into making fuel cells small and practical continues.

LIGHTER THAN AIR

A propane flame heats the air inside a modern hot-air balloon to make the balloon rise

In 1766, Henry Cavendish discovered that his "inflammable air" was seven times lighter than air. Tiberius Cavallo, an Italian-born scientist living in England, followed up Cavendish's discovery. He succeeded in blowing hydrogen into soap bubbles, making them rise. He thought that if enough hydrogen could be captured in a container, the container would be able to lift a man off the ground. However, at the time, there was no known way to capture hydrogen. It escaped from every container Cavallo tried.

French brothers, Anne-Jean and Marie-Noel Robert, were more successful. They applied varnish to thin silk, making a large, flexible container that kept hydrogen trapped inside.

Balloons

The work of Cavendish, Cavallo, and the Robert brothers led to the work of two more brothers, the Montgolfiers of France, who now get the credit for inventing the balloon in 1783. The two brothers, Jacques Étienne and Joseph Michel, didn't use hydrogen at first. Instead, they used heated air inside a varnished silk bag.

When molecules of air are heated, they move around more than they do when cool, and they take up more space. Therefore, a specific volume of hot air contains fewer molecules than the same volume of cool air. The hot air weighs less and so it rises through the cool air around it.

By heating the air in their balloon, the Montgolfiers made their balloon rise. However, as soon as the air in the balloon cooled, the great bag sank back to the ground. Despite that, the Montgolfiers succeeded in astonishing French King Louis XVI by sending a goose, a rooster, and a sheep up into the atmosphere riding together in a basket fastened beneath the balloon.

French scientist J.A.C. Charles was asked by the French Academy of Sciences to investigate the Montgolfiers' invention. Within days, he solved the cooling-air problem by filling a balloon with hydrogen, a process he had learned about from Cavendish's writings. Charles built a balloon 4 meters (13 ft) in diameter and sent it, unmanned, into the air. When it was found later, it had traveled 26 kilometers (16 mi) in 45 minutes.

Challenged by the idea of people being carried by such a balloon, Charles added a large net covering to the balloon and attached the net to a basket beneath the balloon. He also added a valve at the top of the balloon so that the pilot could release gas when he wanted to land. As the hydrogen gas in the bag escaped, the balloon sank back to earth.

On December 1, 1783, Charles and one of the Robert brothers made the first manned flight in a hydrogen-filled balloon.

An artist's idea of an early hot-air balloon being prepared for liftoff in front of an excited crowd

Ballooning quickly turned into a popular sport. The sight of the strange devices in the air often sent terror into the hearts of peasants in the countryside. Hot air and hydrogen remained the basic methods of lifting people into the air in balloons until helium, the second-lightest gas, began to be used in the twentieth century.

Hydrogen in Airships

The Robert brothers quickly applied what they had learned to the development of an elongated balloon that would move through the air more easily than a round shape does. The problem was how to propel the vehicle forward. Some experimenters tried to have people in a basket turn a propeller with handcranks. Such airships got off the ground because they were filled with hot air or hydrogen, but the people very quickly grew tired of cranking. The first real airship had to await the development of a suitable engine.

In 1852, Henri Giffard attached a steam engine to an elongated hydrogen-filled craft and flew at 9.7 kilometers (6 mi) per hour. Thirty-two years later, using a battery-powered engine,

Charles Rénard and A. C. Krebs succeeded in flying a hydrogen-filled airship and maneuvering it back to its starting point. These were the first steerable airships, or dirigibles.

Graf (Count) Ferdinand von Zeppelin, working in Germany about 1900, built an airship that had a rigid, fabric-covered structure. Hydrogen-filled bags inside the airframe provided lift for his airship, and engines mounted outside the airship propelled it forward. His company carried passengers in airships throughout Germany for several years before World War I (1914–1918). He did not live long enough to see his partner, Hugo Eckener, turn the airships—which he called Zeppelins in the count's honor—into an elegant, relaxed means of transportation. The *Graf Zeppelin,* carried passengers completely around the world in 1929.

Eckener's Zeppelins encountered an important problem. As the fuel—a mixture of gasoline and benzol, which also comes from petroleum—was burned by the engines, the craft lost weight and rose higher than the pilot intended.

The pilots of the Zeppelin Company were ordered to release 1 cubic meter (36 cu ft) of hydrogen for every kilogram of fuel burned. But the engineers had a better idea. Instead of releasing the hydrogen to the air, they piped it into the engines, where it was burned along with the fuel, thus increasing engine power. On one major 9,700-kilometer (6,000-mi) test of the idea, they found that 14 percent less fuel was burned when released hydrogen was added to the mix.

Unfortunately, throughout all this development, one fact about hydrogen never changed: the gas is explosive. It was always handled very carefully. No cigarettes or other fires were allowed anywhere near the hydrogen supply. The Zeppelin Company tried to obtain helium gas, which is almost as light as hydrogen and is not explosive. However, the helium supplies of the world were in the hands of Americans and Canadians, who were unwilling to sell helium to Germany.

The explosion of the hydrogen-filled Zeppelin Hindenburg in 1937 marked the end of the era of luxury travel aboard airships.

On May 6, 1937, the Zeppelin Company's new luxury airship, *Hindenburg,* was coming in to land at Lakehurst, New Jersey, with 97 passengers and crew members on board. A ground crew of almost 250 men waited for cables and ropes to be tossed down so that the huge ship—almost 245 meters (804 ft) long—could be helped to dock.

As the greatest luxury airship ever built approached, a small explosion was heard by the watchers. Suddenly the ship got off balance, and in making the correction, a hydrogen bag, or cell, tore open and the explosive gas began to vent. A spark, perhaps from static electricity, ignited the gas, and one by one, the gas cells, containing 200,000 cubic meters (7,063,000 cu ft) of hydrogen, exploded, and the great ship sank to the ground in flames. Amazingly, only thirty-five of the people on board were killed, but the use of airships for travel ended that day.

Today, advertising blimps are often seen in the skies as they televise sporting events from the air. Such blimps are filled with helium, which is not flammable and therefore not as dangerous as hydrogen, so perhaps regular airship travel will someday be possible again.

A HYDROGEN CATALOG

Health and Fashion

Dihydrogen oxide, H_2O, is better known as water. But if one more atom of oxygen is added to the water molecule, it becomes hydrogen peroxide, H_2O_2. By itself, hydrogen peroxide is a thick, colorless liquid that can explode. But if only a little is diluted (thinned out) in water, the liquid can be used as an antiseptic, or bacteria killer, to clean cuts on the skin. People who have just had their ears pierced may use hydrogen peroxide to clean the holes until they heal.

Diluted H_2O_2 is also used to take color out of hair to prepare it before dyeing it a different color. The chemical softens the cortex, or central shaft, of the hair, which allows color to enter it. It also removes color, or melanin, from the hair, bleaching it so that lighter colors can be used on once-dark hair.

A mixture of hair dye and hydrogen peroxide modifies the hair so that the new color stays trapped in it.

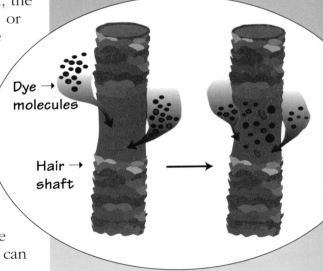

Dye → molecules

Hair → shaft

43

Until hydrogen peroxide was discovered in 1818, cotton and linen clothing usually had to be dyed different colors or used in their natural off-white color. By using H_2O_2, manufacturers could bleach fabrics pure white.

Working with Cold

Scottish physicist James Dewar was fascinated by liquefied gases, which were made by cooling gases to low temperatures. He wanted to be able to preserve liquefied gases for long periods of time. Usually they turned to gas again as soon as they began to warm up.

In 1892, Dewar invented a special bottle to store liquid oxygen. It had two steel walls with an open space between them from which all gases were sucked out. Such a completely empty space is called a vacuum. Heat needs air molecules to move through, so when the air was removed from the space, heat could not move through it. The vacuum prevented the temperature of the air from turning the liquid inside the bottle back into a gas. Today, Dewar's invention is called a Dewar flask, a vacuum bottle, or, more popularly, a thermos bottle, after the company that sold them to the public.

Having achieved a way to preserve liquefied gases, Dewar set about trying to liquefy hydrogen, a goal that had defeated previous efforts by other scientists. He used the principle that when a gas expands, its temperature drops. He built an apparatus that allowed a small container of com-

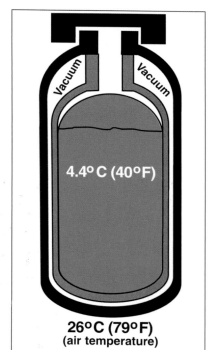

26°C (79°F)
(air temperature)

A Dewar flask keeps heat from moving into or out of the substance inside the container.

pressed hydrogen gas to stand in the stream of another gas that was released from a second container. As the second gas escaped, its lower temperature cooled the vial of hydrogen gas. He then used that cooled hydrogen as the expanding gas to cool another vial of hydrogen. He did this procedure over and over, with each stage cooling some hydrogen a little more. Finally, in 1898, Dewar succeeded in cooling the hydrogen gas enough to turn it into a liquid. The following year, he became the first person to freeze hydrogen into a solid.

A Blast of Heat

One way of using hydrogen in industry is the oxyhydrogen torch. Flames from this torch can reach a temperature of about 2,400°C (4,352°F), which is hot enough to melt many metals that can't be melted in any other way. More recently, however, the oxyhydrogen torch has been replaced by the oxyacetylene torch. Acetylene (C_2H_2) is a flammable gas that burns hotter when mixed with oxygen. An oxyacetylene flame can reach a temperature of around 3,314°C (6,000°F).

Plastics

Plastics are generally made from petroleum products, which are hydrocarbons. Plastics manufacturers move the various atoms around in the petroleum molecules to achieve the effect they want. Certain hydrocarbon molecules called monomers can be combined into long strings called polymers (*mono* means "one," and *poly* means "many".) Many of the plastic materials we are all familiar with are polymers.

Vinyl plastic is used for seat covers and raincoats, and it was used for phonograph records. Vinyl is made in a chemical reaction that removes a hydrogen atom from ethylene (C_2H_4) and replaces it with a chlorine atom. Then the molecule is repeated over and over in long chains to make polyvinyl chloride (PVC).

The Lone Atom

Lone hydrogen atoms may be playing an important role in saving the ozone layer over the Earth, and thus protecting living things from dangerous ultraviolet rays from the sun. About 25 kilometers (15.5 mi) above the earth is a layer of ozone molecules—oxygen molecules made out of three atoms (O_3) of oxygen instead of the two (O_2) in normal atmospheric oxygen. These special molecules have the ability to absorb the ultraviolet rays in sunlight, preventing them from reaching Earth.

In recent years, the ozone layer has been getting thinner because of a group of chemicals invented and used by humans. The chemicals are chlorofluorocarbons (CFCs), a combination of chlorine, fluorine, and carbon. They are nonreactive and have long been used in spray cans as propellants, and in automobile air conditioners, refrigerators, and freezers as coolants. Chlorofluorocarbons are also used as the gas that makes polystyrene plastic foam into a strong but lightweight material.

It wasn't until the 1980s that scientists discovered that CFCs were not as harmless in the atmosphere as they seemed. Instead, they rise to the ozone layer where CFC molecules are split apart by sunlight, which releases some of the chlorine. The freed chlorine reacts with the O_3 to produce chlorine oxide and oxygen.

$$Cl + O_3 \rightarrow ClO + O_2$$

The chlorine oxide then reacts further to produce chlorine and normal oxygen:

$$2ClO \rightarrow 2Cl + O_2$$

As you can see in the reaction above, the chlorine is regenerated after it destroys an ozone molecule. One chlorine atom can thus destroy thousands of ozone molecules before it is itself finally made inactive by chemical reactions. Most of the nations of the world have agreed that the specific kind of CFC that is causing the trouble can no longer be used. However, it will be many decades before all the chlorine already in the stratosphere is used up and the ozone layer stops decomposing.

How is hydrogen playing a role in all this? When the problem became clear, chemists went back to the laboratory. They developed chemicals that are similar to CFCs but also have a hydrogen atom added to their molecular structures. These chemicals are called hydrochlorofluorocarbons, or HCFCs for short.

The ozone layer is a belt of O_3 molecules around Earth that protects living things from the harmful radiation of the sun.

Because of the ease with which the HCFCs react with chemicals in the atmosphere, fewer of these molecules reach the stratosphere. HCFCs do deliver some chlorine to the ozone layer, so they will not be used any longer than necessary while non-chlorine gases are developed. The aim is to replace all such chemicals with others containing only hydrogen, carbon, and fluorine.

The Last Trace of Earth

The outermost portion of Earth's atmosphere—at an altitude between approximately 322 and 483 kilometers (200 and 300 mi)—consists of a belt of hydrogen atoms. Even though lower in the atmosphere, hydrogen gas is diatomic, hydrogen exists as individual atoms at the higher altitude. Above that belt, what remains of the atmosphere, called the exosphere, is the area where gaseous atoms are easily flung off into space. There are so few atoms of any kind in that region that they don't bang into each other as they move around. Instead, they often gain enough velocity—10.9 kilometers (6.8 mi) per second—to escape the Earth's gravitational pull.

The Shadow of Things to Come

Geologists who study earthquakes and volcanic eruptions have long tried to forecast when such catastrophic events are likely to happen. Since 1985, they have found that before major earthquakes take place, large quantities of hydrogen gas may be released from within the Earth. Several days before Mount St. Helens in Washington state erupted in 1980, geologists noticed hydrogen gas escaping from the ground. However, hydrogen is not always released before volcanic eruptions, so looking for it is not always a guard against coming disaster.

Hydrogen and the MRI

A machine called an MRI has become very important in helping doctors determine what is wrong with many patients. MRI, which means Magnetic Resonance Imaging, can "see" changes inside soft body tissues, which means there is no need to operate on a patient in order to make a diagnosis of an internal disorder. X rays reveal only the hard, calcium-filled bony tissues of the body.

The hydrogen protons in the human body normally lie in all sorts of random directions. The MRI

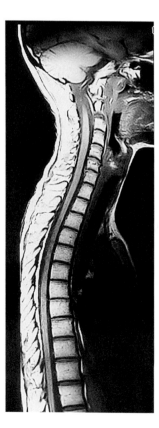

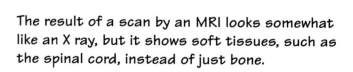

The result of a scan by an MRI looks somewhat like an X ray, but it shows soft tissues, such as the spinal cord, instead of just bone.

gives a magnetic burst that makes the protons rearrange themselves in one direction. Then, radio waves are sent through the body. The radio energy knocks the protons out of alignment. As they settle back into alignment again, they give off a radio signal that can be measured. Each kind of tissue gives a different kind of signal, which a computer changes into a picture of the tissue.

Speeding Up Protons

Particle accelerators (sometimes called atom smashers) are huge devices that use electricity to make electrons or protons move faster and faster. As they speed up, these particles acquire more energy. When these high-energy particles smash into an atom, the atom's nucleus breaks up into particles that are even smaller than protons and neutrons. These are subatomic particles, such as quarks and neutrinos. Gradually, over the decades, nuclear scientists have been able to locate and describe the basic subparticles that make up all matter as well as the forces that hold them together.

The earliest particle accelerators used protons from hydrogen atoms as the particles to be accelerated. Today, such protons are still used, but protons from other atoms are used, too. An important use of accelerators today is to create radioactive isotopes of various elements for use in medicine.

Tracing with Tritium

An isotope of hydrogen can be used to locate a tumor inside the body. Tritium, the hydrogen isotope with two neutrons and one proton in its nucleus, is used in working with a Positron Emission Transaxial Tomography (PETT)—a machine used to find brain tumors. The isotope is injected into the bloodstream, where it makes its way to the brain. It is caught by tumor tissue and can be photographed, showing the tumor's density and size.

A PETT machine with its cover off (right), while a technician changes the settings. Below is a PETT scan of the brain of a smoker (bottom) and a nonsmoker (top). The colors show different compounds within the brain.

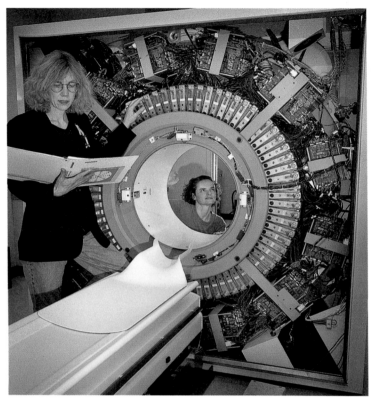

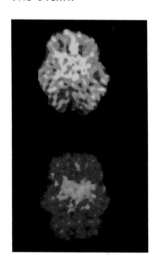

Different compounds within the brain, revealing other illnesses, can also be photographed.

Tritium tracers are also used in oil pipelines, which carry a wide variety of different products of petroleum. At the petroleum refinery, different products are put into a single pipeline, but radioactive isotopes are placed between the products. When a company is ready to remove the product it wants—perhaps a specific type of motor oil—from a pipe, the receiving company can detect where the specific product begins and ends by the presence of the tracer isotopes.

Hidden Treasure

In 1935, French husband-and-wife physicists Frédéric and Irène Joliot-Curie won the Nobel Prize in Chemistry for research that they hoped might lead to a nuclear chain reaction (and perhaps a bomb). In their research, they had developed the world's largest supply of heavy water, or deuterium oxide (D_2O). But their work was stopped when Hitler's German troops overran France in 1940. The Joliot-Curies managed to smuggle their heavy-water supply out of France ahead of the German soldiers. It remained safely hidden from the Germans throughout World War II, and when the fighting was over, the scientists retrieved the rare chemical.

France used the heavy water in building its first nuclear power plant. In a nuclear chain reaction, neutrons are released from atomic nuclei. During an atomic-bomb explosion, those neutrons move with incredible speed. But in a nuclear power plant, the neutrons need to be moderated, or slowed down. Heavy water has the ability to slow—but not stop—neutrons to speeds at which they can be captured and controlled.

The Dangerous Bubble

In most nuclear power plants, the atomic core has water circulating around it to keep it from reaching dangerously high temperatures. In March 1979, at the Three Mile Island nuclear power plant near Harrisburg, Pennsylvania, some of the coolant water was lost and the core overheated. In doing so, the high temperature of the casing of the reactor caused the water to decompose, and a huge bubble of hydrogen gas formed inside the reactor.

The bubble of hydrogen prevented the coolant water from reaching vital parts of the reactor core. Some radioactive gases escaped into the air. Some of the coolant water, which was radioactive, spilled into the Susquehanna River. Almost 50,000 people had to be evacuated from the immediate area of the nuclear power plant. Thousands more had to stay indoors for many days to keep from being contaminated by radiation in the atmosphere. No new nuclear power plants have been constructed in the United States since the Three-Mile Island accident.

The Hydrogen Bomb

President Harry Truman ordered the development of the hydrogen bomb in January 1950 and the bomb was first tested in 1952. The massive explosion got its energy from lightweight hydrogen atomic nuclei being fused together. This fusion reaction produced a thousand times more heat, light, and energy than the atomic bombs dropped on Japan in 1945 at the end of World War II. The atomic bomb worked by a fission reaction, splitting nuclei apart.

An explosion testing the power of a hydrogen bomb was carried out in 1952.

Fusion in Our Future

Nuclear fission works by splitting the nuclei of atoms apart, a process that releases great amounts of energy. Even more energy can be derived from nuclear fusion. This is the same process that takes place in the hydrogen bomb and in the stars.

However, nuclear fusion in the stars releases a great deal more heat than science can tame. In our sun, for example, it is estimated that the temperature is at least 15,000,000°C (27,000,000°F), and the hydrogen at the center of that stellar body is under a pressure of almost 3 trillion pounds per square inch. Those conditions make hydrogen as dense as uranium, the densest metal on Earth.

Scientists are hoping to develop a way for nuclear fusion to occur at room temperature. The ability to control such fusion would supply all human energy requirements on the Earth forever. We would not run out of fuels.

One design for controlled fusion, called the Tokamak reactor, was designed by Russian scientists several decades ago. It holds ionized hydrogen in a magnetic field while it is heated enough to fuse hydrogen nuclei. Another controlled-fusion experiment uses lasers aimed at the point where a small pellet of a frozen isotope of hydrogen is dropped. The pressure and heat exerted by the lasers causes the isotopes to become hot enough to fuse nuclei.

Both of these controlled-fusion devices are still experimental, and they use more energy than they produce. In addition, they use radioactive isotopes of hydrogen to achieve their purpose, while any practical device would have to use common hydrogen.

If scientists ever succeed in achieving controlled fusion, our future world could be powered by hydrogen isotopes found naturally in our most common natural resource—water. The sea could provide enough fusion fuel to supply the people of Earth with energy for a million years.

Fueling Future Transportation

Different fuels give off different amounts of energy depending on how much hydrogen is in the material. When burned, hydrogen gives off almost four times as much energy as carbon does. Gasoline, like all hydrocarbons, contains much hydrogen.

In an automobile gasoline engine, fuel is mixed with oxygen inside a cylinder. As the mixture explodes, it drives a piston that connects to a crankshaft, turning it. Several pistons move back and forth in a continuous flow of explosions. This flow turns the crankshaft that connects to the wheels, keeping them turning. When pure hydrogen is used as the fuel, the engine works exactly the same way, but the explosions don't produce as much heat as gasoline—a hydrocarbon—does. But hydrogen burns cleanly, giving off very little air pollution.

In his last novel, *The Mysterious Island* (1874), Jules Verne, the "father of science fiction," proposes that the coal supplies of the world might run out. One character suggests that future machinery might be run by "water decomposed into its primitive elements, and decomposed doubtless, by electricity, which will then have become a powerful and manageable force." Verne was way ahead of his time.

Starting about 1920, especially in Great Britain and Germany, various writers and scientists began to explore the use of hydrogen for energy. Some enthusiasts built their own vehicles to run on hydrogen. British scientist J.B.S. Haldane proposed using wind power to produce the electricity needed to separate oxygen from water by electrolysis.

In the 1930s, German engineer Rudolf Erren converted many different vehicles to run on hydrogen fuel as well as gasoline as the driver desired. He recognized that an important problem with submarines was that their movement underwater could be detected by the string of exhaust bubbles that followed them. He

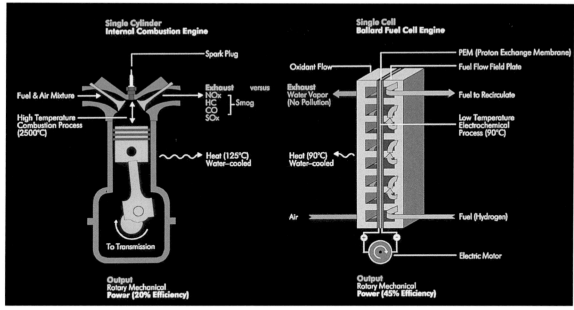

A comparison of one cylinder in an internal combustion engine that burns gasoline (left) and a single fuel cell (right). An array of fuel cells used to power a vehicle is shown on page 57

developed a submarine that burned liquid oxygen and liquid hydrogen. The exhaust from burning these two materials was, of course, water, so there was no bubble wake. The British expressed interest in the sub, but did not follow up the work. They did not know that Britain and Germany would be at war with each other in a few years. Germany was not able to make the idea practical for its wartime submarines.

After World War II (1939–1945), research into hydrogen as a fuel slowed. The National Advisory Committee for Aeronautics (NACA, the forerunner of NASA, the U.S. space agency) proved that airplanes could run on hydrogen. But they did nothing with the results of their work.

In the 1960s, the major automobile companies began to work on hydrogen-fueled cars, especially as concern for the environment grew. Again, nothing happened until the early 1970s, when people began to be concerned about running out of petroleum. As long waiting lines formed at gasoline pumps, research into hydrogen as a fuel was renewed.

Today, hydrogen-fueled cars are on the road again. But they are few and are still experimental. The major problem is that storing hydrogen takes up so much more space than gasoline. For example, a car with a 75-liter (20-gal) gasoline tank would need to have a 295-liter (78-gal) hydrogen tank to travel the same distance on a tankful of fuel. The hydrogen itself weighs much less than the gasoline, but it must be stored in a heavy tank to keep it from expanding. Also, such tanks could explode during a crash. Automotive scientists are looking at other methods by which vehicles can carry hydrogen.

One method is to cool the hydrogen gas to a liquid and keep it in Dewar flasks. The hydrogen would take up a lot less space, but "thermos bottles" for liquid hydrogen would be fairly heavy and expensive.

Another idea calls for combining hydrogen with remarkable substances called hydrides. Hydrides are basically metals or metalloids combined with hydrogen. They look like tiny metal granules, but they absorb huge quantities of hydrogen like sponges because the hydrogen atoms fill spaces in the structure of the hydrides. When heated, the hydrides give off the hydrogen. Vehicles using hydride-stored hydrogen have been tested for almost twenty years.

The best answer for the future is using fuel cells to make electricity to directly power a vehicle. In 1997, Daimler-Benz of Germany showed a passenger car with a fuel cell. It uses methanol, or methyl alcohol (CH_3OH), as the source of hydrogen. Soon afterward, a company in the United States succeeded in

An array of fuel cells (the vertical devices lined up at right) is packed inside the engine of an experimental bus produced by a Canadian company.

making a fuel cell that uses gasoline to make electricity instead of burning the fuel as internal combustion engines do. Using gasoline will still require that petroleum be taken from the earth, but an electric car would go twice as far on 4 liters (1 gal) of gasoline as a car with an internal combustion engine. Just as important, since the gasoline itself is not burned, pollutants that harm our cities and crops would not be produced.

The gasoline fuel cell does not yet solve the problem of using up natural resources. However, it may be a useful in-between stage before the fuel cell that runs on water is perfected.

Hydrogen in Brief

Name: hydrogen, from Greek words meaning "water-forming"
Symbol: H
Discoverer: Henry Cavendish
Atomic number: 1
Atomic weight (mass number): 1.00797
Electrons in single shell: 1
Group: often put in Group 1 because it has only 1 electron in a single shell. However, it does not resemble the other elements in that group. Sometimes also put at the top of Group 7.
Usual characteristics: nonmetallic, tasteless, odorless, colorless gas; lightest element known
Density (mass per unit volume): 0.00008375 grams per cubic meter at 20°C (68°F); least dense—only about one-fourteenth the density of air; least dense element
Melting point (freezing point): −259.14°C (−434.45°F)
Boiling point (liquefaction point): −252.8°C (−422.8°F)
Abundance:
    Universe: most abundant (60.4%)
    Earth: one of many totaling only 1.4%
    Earth's crust: 10th most abundant element, but makes up only 0.1%
    Earth's atmosphere: 0.00005%, 9th most abundant element in dry air
    Human body: more atoms than all other elements combined; by weight, 60 percent of the body is water
Stable isotopes: protium, the main form of hydrogen, and deuterium
Radioactive isotope: tritium

GLOSSARY

acid: definitions vary, but basically an acid is a corrosive substance that gives up a positive hydrogen ion, H+, equal to a proton when dissolved in water; indicates less than 7 on the pH scale because of its large number of hydrogen ions

alchemy: the combination of science, religion, and magic that preceded chemistry

alkali: a substance, such as a hydroxide or carbonate of an alkali metal, that, when dissolved in water, causes an increase in the hydroxide ion (OH-) concentration, thus forming a basic solution.

anion: an ion with a negative charge

atom: the smallest amount of an element that exhibits the properties of the element, consisting of protons, electrons, and (usually) neutrons

base: a substance that accepts a hydrogen ion, H+, when dissolved in water; indicates higher than 7 on the pH scale because of its small number of hydrogen ions

boiling point: the temperature at which a liquid at normal pressure evaporates into a gas, or a solid changes directly (sublimes) into a gas; also, the temperature at which a gas condenses into a liquid or solid

bond: the attractive force linking atoms together in a molecule or crystal

catalyst: a substance that causes or speeds a chemical reaction without itself being used up or consumed in the reaction

cation: an ion with a positive charge

chemical reaction: a change or transformation in a substance involving the electrons of the chemical elements making up the substance

combustion: burning, or rapid combination of a substance with oxygen, usually producing heat and light

compound: a substance formed by two or more chemical elements bound together by chemical means

covalent bond: a link between two atoms made by the atoms sharing electrons

decompose: to break down a substance into its components

density: the amount of material in a given volume, or space; mass per unit volume; often stated as grams per cubic centimeter (g/cm³)

diatomic: made up of two atoms

dissolve: to spread evenly throughout the volume of another substance

distillation: the process in which a liquid is heated until it evaporates and the gas is collected and condensed back into a liquid in another container; often used to separate mixtures into their different components

DNA: deoxyribonucleic acid, a chemical in the nucleus of each living cell, which carries genetic information

double bond: the sharing of two pairs of electrons between two atoms in a molecule

electrode: a device such as a metal plate that conducts electrons into or out of a solution or battery

electrolysis: the decomposition of a substance by electricity

electrolyte: a substance that conducts electricity when dissolved in water or when liquefied

element: a substance that cannot be split chemically into simpler substances that maintain the same characteristics. Each of the 103 naturally occurring chemical elements is made up of atoms of the same kind.

enzyme: one of many complex proteins that act as biological catalysts in the body

evaporate: to change from a liquid to a gas

fossil fuel: petroleum, natural gas, or coal, all of which are formed from the remains of plants and animals

gas: a state of matter in which the atoms or molecules move freely, matching the shape and volume of the container holding it

group: a vertical column in the Periodic Table, with each element having similar physical and chemical characteristics; also called chemical family

half-life: the period of time required for half of a radioactive element to decay

hydrocarbon: a compound made of only carbon and hydrogen

ion: an atom or molecule that has acquired an electric charge by gaining or losing one or more electrons

ionic bond: a link between two atoms made by one atom taking one or more electrons from the other, giving them opposite electrical charges, which holds them together

isotope: an atom with a different number of neutrons in its nucleus from other atoms of the same element

mass number: the total of protons and neutrons in the nucleus of an atom

melting point: the temperature at which a solid becomes a liquid

metal: a chemical element that conducts electricity, usually shines, or reflects light, is dense, and can be shaped. About three-quarters of the naturally occurring elements are metals.

metalloid: a chemical element that has some characteristics of a metal and some of a nonmetal; includes some elements in groups 13 through 17 in the Periodic Table

molecule: the smallest amount of a substance that has the characteristics of the substance and consists of two or more atoms

neutral: 1) having neither acidic or basic properties; 2) having no electrical charge

neutron: a subatomic particle within the nucleus of all atoms except protium, the most common isotope of hydrogen; has no electric charge

nonmetal: a chemical element that does not conduct electricity, is not dense, and is too brittle to be worked. Nonmetals easily form ions, and they include some elements in groups 14 through 17 and all of group 18 in the Periodic Table.

nucleus: 1) the central part of an atom, which has a positive electrical charge from its one or more protons; the nuclei of all atoms except hydrogen also include electrically neutral neutrons; 2) the central portion of most living cells that controls the activities of the cells and contains genetic material

oxidation: the loss of electrons during a chemical reaction, which occurs in conjunction with reduction; need not necessarily involve the element oxygen

pH: a measure of the acidity of a substance, on a scale of 0 to 14, with 7 being neutral. The abbreviation pH stands for "potential of hydrogen."

photosynthesis: in green plants, the process by which carbon dioxide and water, in the presence of light, are turned into sugars

protein: a complex biological chemical made by the linking of many amino acids

proton: a subatomic particle within the nucleus of all atoms; has a positive electric charge

radical: an atom or molecule that contains an unpaired electron

radioactive: spontaneously emitting high-energy particles

reduction: the gain of electrons during a chemical reaction; occurs in conjunction with oxidation

salt: any compound that, with water, results from the neutralization of an acid by a base. In common usage, sodium chloride (table salt).

shell: a region surrounding the nucleus of an atom in which one or more electrons can occur. The inner shell can hold a maximum of two electrons; others may hold eight or more. If an atom's outer, or valence, shell does not hold its maximum number of electrons, the atom is subject to chemical reactions.

solid: a state of matter in which the shape of the collection of atoms or molecules does not depend on the container

solution: a mixture in which one substance is evenly distributed throughout another

sublime: to change directly from a solid to a gas without becoming a liquid first

triple bond: the sharing of three pairs of electrons between two atoms in a molecule

ultraviolet: electromagnetic radiation which has a wavelength shorter than visible light

valence electron: an electron located in the outer shell of an atom, available to participate in chemical reactions

For Further Information

BOOKS

Atkins, P. W. *The Periodic Kingdom: A Journey into the Land of the Chemical Elements.* NY: Basic Books, 1995

Heiserman, David L. *Exploring Chemical Elements and Their Compounds.* Blue Ridge Summit, PA: Tab Books, 1992

Hoffman, Roald, and Vivian Torrence. *Chemistry Imagined: Reflections on Science.* Washington, DC: Smithsonian Institution Press, 1993

Newton, David E. *Chemical Elements.* Venture Books. Danbury, CT: Franklin Watts, 1994

Yount, Lisa. *Antoine Lavoisier: Founder of Modern Chemistry.* "Great Minds of Science" series. Springfield, NJ: Enslow Publishers, 1997

CD-ROM

Discover the Elements: The Interactive Periodic Table of the Chemical Elements. Paradigm Interactive, Greensboro, NC, 1995

INTERNET SITES

Note that useful sites on the Internet can change and even disappear. If the following site addresses do not work, use a search engine that you find useful, such as Yahoo:

       http://www.yahoo.com

or AltaVista:

       http://altavista.digital.com

A very thorough listing of the major characteristics, uses, and compounds of all the chemical elements can be found at a site called WebElements:

       http://www.shef.ac.uk/~chem/web-elements/

A Canadian site on the Nature of the Environment includes a large section on the elements in the various Earth systems:

       http://www.cent.org/geo12/geo12/htm

Colored photos of various molecules, cells, and biological systems can be viewed at:

       http://www.clarityconnect.com-/webpages/cramer/PictureIt/welcome.htm

Many subjects are covered on WWW Virtual Library. It also includes a useful collection of links to other sites:

       http://www.earthsystems.org/Environment/shtml

INDEX